No part of this book may be reproduced, distributed, or transmitted in any form or by any means, including electronic, mechanical, photocopying, recording, or otherwise, without the prior written permission of the publisher.

Culture lover is the copyright owner of the content of this book and does not permit the use of the content of this book by any other person or entity. Using the content of this book without permission will constitute copyright infringement and Culture lover has the right to take legal action for copyright infringement.

TABLE OF CONTENTS

SPACE

Space

Space is vast and empty. It would take light 93 million miles to travel from one end of the Milky Way galaxy to the other.

The sun is a star. It is the center of our solar system and is made up of mostly hydrogen and helium.

The Moon is the Earth's only natural satellite. It is about one-quarter the size of the Earth and is made up of mostly rock and dust.

The Milky Way galaxy is a spiral galaxy. It is home to about 100 billion stars, including our sun.

The Andromeda Galaxy is the closest major galaxy to our Milky Way. It is about 2.5 million light-years away.

The universe is expanding. This means that the distance between galaxies is getting larger over time.

Space

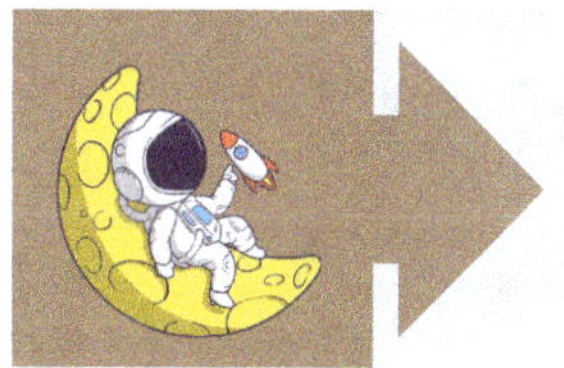

The Sun is a big ball of hot gas that keeps our planet warm and gives us light during the day.

Jupiter is the largest planet in our solar system, and it has a big red spot on its surface called the Great Red Spot.

Saturn is known for its stunning rings made up of ice and rocks that orbit around the planet.

Mars is often called the "Red Planet" because its surface is covered in reddish dust and rocks.

Venus is the hottest planet in our solar system, even hotter than Mercury, which is closer to the Sun.

The International Space Station (ISS) is a giant laboratory in space where astronauts live and work for months at a time.

Space

Astronauts have to wear spacesuits outside their spacecraft to protect them from extreme temperatures and lack of air in space.

The Hubble Space Telescope takes amazing pictures of distant galaxies and helps scientists learn more about the universe.

Neil Armstrong was the first person to walk on the Moon during the Apollo 11 mission in 1969.

The Milky Way is the name of our galaxy, and it contains billions of stars, including our Sun.

The atmosphere is the layer of gases surrounding a planet, and it protects us from harmful radiation from the Sun.

Astronomers use telescopes to observe distant objects in space and gather data about galaxies, stars, and planets.

Space

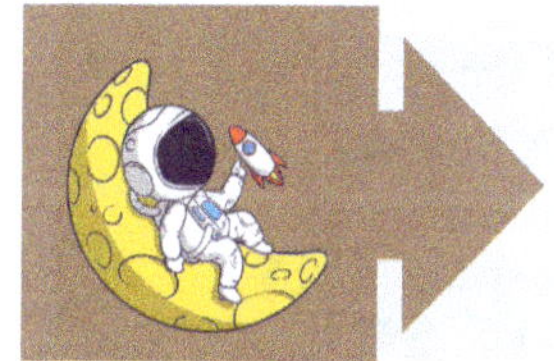

Astronauts have to exercise regularly in space to prevent their muscles and bones from becoming weak due to the lack of gravity.

Black holes are incredibly dense objects with such strong gravity that nothing, not even light, can escape from them.

The Mars atmosphere is very thin, mostly composed of carbon dioxide, making it impossible for us to breathe without specialized equipment.

The first American woman to go to space was Sally Ride in 1983.

Astronauts need to sleep in special sleeping bags strapped to the walls so they don't float around.

The word "astronomy" comes from the Greek words "astron," meaning star, and "nomos," meaning law.

Space

Jupiter has the shortest day of all the planets; it completes one rotation in less than 10 hours.

The first animal to orbit the Earth was a dog named Laika, sent by the Soviet Union in 1957.

The temperature in outer space can be extremely cold, reaching hundreds of degrees below zero.

The Sun is so big that you could fit about 1.3 million Earths inside it!

The first animals to go into space were fruit flies in 1947!

Nebulas are massive clouds of gas and dust where new stars are born.

Space

Planets come in different sizes. For example, Earth is smaller than Jupiter, but it is bigger than Mars.

Did you know that space is a vacuum, which means it is completely empty of air and sound? That's why astronauts need spacesuits to breathe!

The Earth is the only known planet to have life, and it is covered with oceans, forests, mountains, and deserts.

Comets are icy objects that travel through space and leave a glowing trail behind them when they get close to the Sun.

Satellites are objects that orbit around planets and help us with communication, weather forecasts, and even GPS navigation!

Stars are huge balls of hot gas that produce their own light and twinkle in the night sky.

Space

Did you know that Jupiter, the largest planet in our Solar System, has a massive storm called the Great Red Spot?

Neil Armstrong, the first human to step foot on the Moon, famously said, "That's one small step for a man, one giant leap for mankind."

Saturn has beautiful rings made of ice, rock, and dust.

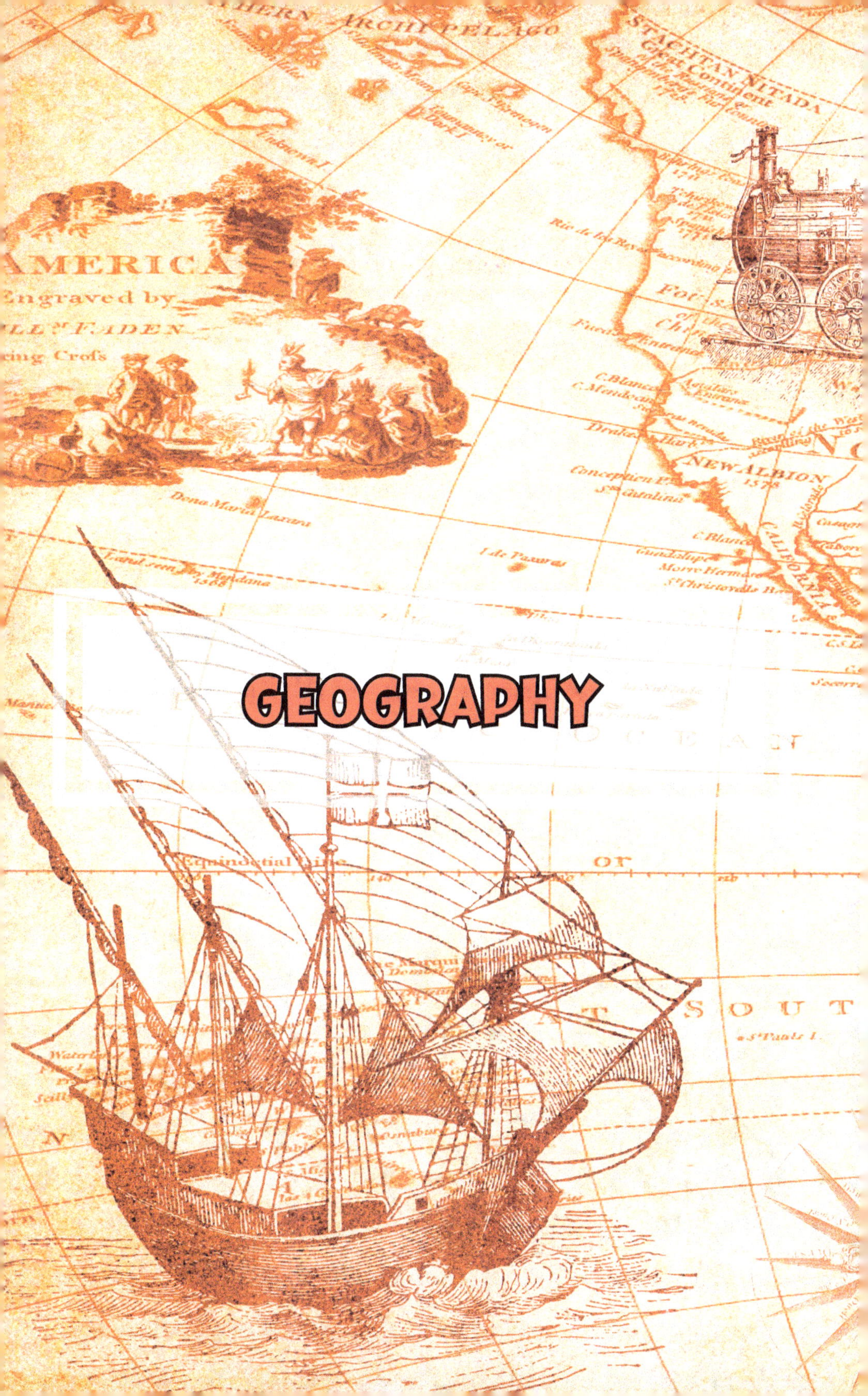

GEOGRAPHY

Geography

The highest mountain on Earth is Mount Everest, and it reaches up into the sky like a giant snow-covered pyramid.

The Great Barrier Reef in Australia is the largest coral reef system in the world, and it's so big that you can see it from space!

The Amazon Rainforest is home to the most diverse range of plant and animal species on the planet, including colorful birds, playful monkeys, and slithering snakes.

Africa is known as the "Cradle of Humanity" because it is believed to be where the first humans originated thousands of years ago.

The Nile River in Egypt is the longest river in the world, and it played a crucial role in the development of ancient Egyptian civilization.

The Sahara Desert in Africa is the largest hot desert in the world, with vast stretches of golden sand and towering sand dunes that seem to go on forever.

Geography

The Great Wall of China is an incredible man-made structure that stretches across thousands of miles, built centuries ago to protect against invasions.

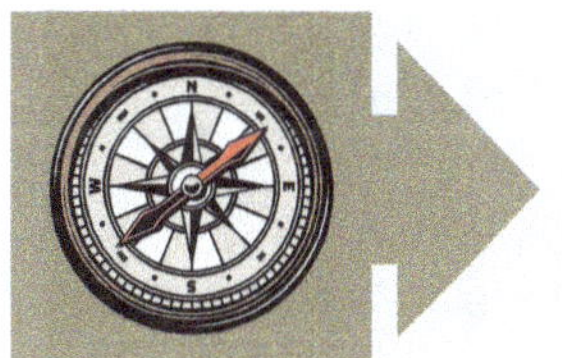

Mount Fuji in Japan is an iconic volcano with a perfectly symmetrical cone shape, often depicted in traditional Japanese art.

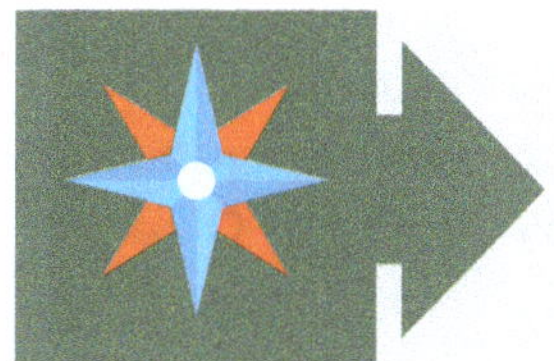

The Eiffel Tower in Paris is an iconic landmark known for its intricate ironwork and panoramic views of the city.

Antarctica is the coldest continent on Earth, covered in ice and inhabited by penguins, seals, and other unique Antarctic animals.

The Taj Mahal in India is a stunning marble mausoleum that was built as a tribute to love, and its beauty attracts millions of visitors each year.

The Caribbean islands are known for their beautiful beaches, crystal-clear waters, and vibrant coral reefs, making them popular vacation destinations.

Geography

The Sydney Opera House in Australia is a famous performing arts venue with its distinctive sail-like design, hosting concerts, theater performances, and more.

The Serengeti National Park in Tanzania is home to the annual migration of millions of wildebeest and other animals, creating a spectacular wildlife spectacle.

The Great Sphinx in Egypt is a massive statue with the body of a lion and the head of a human, guarding the pyramids of Giza.

The Acropolis in Athens, Greece, is an ancient citadel perched on a rocky hilltop, housing historic monuments like the Parthenon.

The Victoria Falls in Africa are one of the Seven Natural Wonders of the World, with a thunderous cascade of water plummeting down a vast gorge.

The Great Rift Valley in East Africa is a massive geological formation stretching thousands of miles, known for its stunning landscapes and diverse wildlife.

Geography

The Colosseum in Rome, Italy, is an ancient amphitheater that once hosted gladiator fights and other spectacles for the entertainment of the Roman people.

The Dead Sea, bordered by Jordan and Israel, is a salty lake where you can effortlessly float on its surface due to its high salt content.

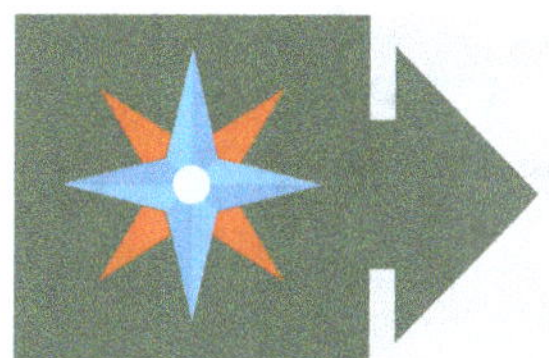

The Amazon Rainforest produces more than 20% of the world's oxygen.

The coldest inhabited place on Earth is Oymyakon, a village in Russia. Temperatures there can drop below -50 (-58 Fahrenheit) degrees Celsius.

The Earth's oceans cover about 71% of the planet's surface.

The Earth's deepest ocean is the Mariana Trench, which is located in the Pacific Ocean.

Geography

Australia is both a country and a continent, and it is the only continent that is also an entire country.

Iceland is known as the "Land of Fire and Ice" because it has both active volcanoes and glaciers.

The Sahara Desert is expanding by about 0.8 kilometers (0.5 miles) each month.

The Andes Mountains in South America are the longest mountain range on land, stretching over 7,000 kilometers (4,350 miles).

The Dead Sea is so salty that no fish or aquatic plants can survive in its waters.

The Maldives is the lowest-lying country in the world, with an average ground level of just 1.5 meters (4.9 feet) above sea level.

Geography

The Great Sphinx of Giza in Egypt has the head of a human and the body of a lion, symbolizing wisdom and strength.

The Gobi Desert, located in Asia, is one of the coldest deserts on Earth and experiences extreme temperature fluctuations.

The Okavango Delta in Botswana is the largest inland delta in the world and attracts a diverse range of wildlife.

The city of Venice in Italy is built on over 100 small islands and is famous for its canals and gondolas.

The Atacama Desert in Chile is one of the driest places on Earth, with some areas never receiving rainfall.

Japan is known as the "Land of the Rising Sun."

Geography

The Grand Canyon in the United States is a massive gorge carved by the Colorado River.

The Netherlands is known for its windmills and tulip fields.

Hawaii is the only U.S. state made up entirely of islands.

Japan is made up of over 6,800 islands.

The Grand Canyon is approximately 277 miles long and 18 miles wide.

The world's smallest country is Vatican City, which is only 0.44 square kilometers in size.

Geography

The world's largest city is Tokyo, Japan, which has a population of over 37 million people.

The world's most spoken language is Mandarin Chinese, which is spoken by over 1.1 billion people.

The world's largest island is Greenland, which is 2,166,086 square kilometers in size.

Mount Fuji in Japan is an active volcano and a symbol of the country.

The Baobab tree, found in Africa, has a trunk that can store water to survive in arid conditions.

The Ganges River in India is considered sacred by Hindus and used for religious ceremonies.

Geography

The Sydney Opera House in Australia is an iconic architectural masterpiece.

The Panama Canal connects the Atlantic Ocean and the Pacific Ocean, allowing ships to avoid a long journey around South America.

The Scottish Highlands are known for their stunning landscapes, including mountains, lochs, and castles.

The Komodo dragon, found in Indonesia, is the largest lizard species on Earth.

The Angkor Wat temple complex in Cambodia is the largest religious monument in the world.

The Angel Falls in Venezuela is the highest waterfall in the world.

Geography

The Petra archaeological site in Jordan is known for its ancient rock-cut architecture.

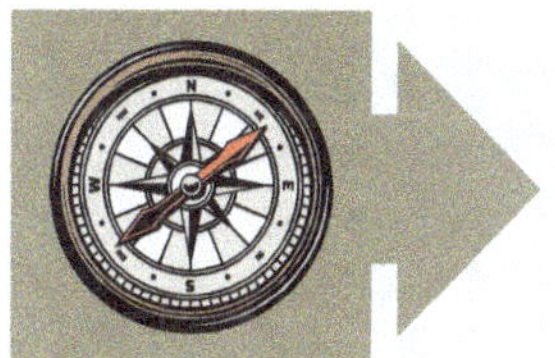

The Machu Picchu in Peru is an ancient Incan citadel nestled in the Andes Mountains.

The Sahara Desert expands across 11 countries in Africa.

The Stonehenge in England is a prehistoric monument made of massive stone blocks.

The Bora Bora Island in French Polynesia is famous for its crystal-clear waters and overwater bungalows.

The Ayers Rock (Uluru) in Australia is a sacred site for the Aboriginal people.

Geography

The country of Liechtenstein is so small that you can walk across it in just a few hours.

There is a pink lake in Australia called Lake Hillier, and scientists are still not sure why it's pink.

In Bolivia, there is a salt flat called Salar de Uyuni that turns into a giant mirror after rain, creating a breathtaking illusion of the sky meeting the ground.

The Zhangye Danxia Landform in China is known for its vibrant and colorful rock formations, resembling a painting come to life.

The Perito Moreno Glacier in Argentina is one of the few glaciers in the world that is still growing instead of shrinking.

The Canary Islands, a Spanish archipelago off the coast of Africa, are named after dogs (canary means dog in Latin) and not the bird.

ANIMALS

Animals

 The blue whale is the largest animal on Earth, even bigger than the largest dinosaur.

 Sloths are known for being the slowest animals in the world, moving at a very leisurely pace.

 The tongue of a blue whale can weigh as much as an elephant.

 Cheetahs are the fastest land animals, capable of reaching speeds up to 70 miles per hour (112 kilometers per hour).

 Elephants are the only mammals that cannot jump.

 A baby kangaroo is called a "joey" and spends its early days in its mother's pouch.

Animals

The hissing cockroach is one of the largest species of cockroaches and can live up to five years.

Male seahorses are responsible for carrying the eggs and giving birth to the young ones.

The tiny hummingbird is the only bird that can fly both forward and backward.

The quokka, a small marsupial from Australia, is often called the happiest animal in the world due to its smile-like expression.

Axolotls, also known as Mexican walking fish, can regenerate lost body parts, including their spinal cord and heart.

The frilled-neck lizard from Australia expands the skin around its neck to intimidate predators.

Animals

The woodpecker's tongue is so long that it wraps around its brain for protection.

The narwhal, a type of whale, has a long tusk-like tooth that can grow up to 10 feet (3 meters) in length.

The platypus, native to Australia, is one of the few mammals that lay eggs instead of giving birth to live young.

The proboscis monkey has a large nose that can grow up to 7 inches (18 centimeters) in length.

The bumblebee bat, also known as Kitti's hog-nosed bat, is the world's smallest mammal, roughly the size of a bumblebee.

The pink fairy armadillo, found in Argentina, is the smallest species of armadillo, measuring only about 4-5 inches (10-13 centimeters) long.

Animals

The axolotl uses external gills to breathe underwater, which give it a distinctive appearance.

The leafy sea dragon, a marine fish, camouflages itself with leaf-like appendages to blend in with seaweed and kelp.

The tufted deer, native to China, has fang-like canines and a distinctive tuft of hair on its forehead.

The fossa, found in Madagascar, is the largest carnivorous mammal on the island and resembles a mix between a cat and a dog.

The pink fairy armadillo spends most of its time underground, using its strong claws to dig burrows.

The blobfish lives in the deep ocean where the pressure is hundreds of times greater than at sea level, which gives it its unique appearance.

Animals

The okapi, found in the rainforests of the Democratic Republic of Congo, is the only known relative of the giraffe.

The star-nosed mole has a nose with 22 tentacle-like appendages that help it detect prey underwater.

The pangolin is the only mammal covered in scales, providing protection against predators.

The slow loris has a toxic bite, secreting venom from glands in its elbows.

The flying squirrel has flaps of skin called patagia that allow it to glide through the air.

The arctic fox changes its fur color from brown to white during winter to blend in with the snowy landscape.

Animals

The binturong, also known as the bearcat, emits a scent similar to popcorn.

The Japanese spider crab has the largest leg span of any arthropod, reaching up to 12 feet.

The shoebill stork has a distinctive shoe-shaped bill that it uses to catch fish.

The world's most common cat is the domestic cat, which is estimated to number over 100 million individuals worldwide.

The world's most vocal cat is the Siamese cat, which is known for its loud meow.

The world's most intelligent animal is the chimpanzee, which is known for its ability to use tools and solve problems.

Animals

There are more than 1,500 different species of bats.

The tongue of a giraffe is dark blue or purple in color.

Honey never spoils. Archaeologists have found pots of honey in ancient Egyptian tombs that are over 3,000 years old and still perfectly edible.

Cows have best friends and become stressed when they are separated.

The average housefly lives for only about 2 to 4 weeks.

Butterflies taste with their feet.

Animals

The slowest fish in the ocean is the seahorse, which swims at about 0.01 miles per hour.

The average lifespan of a squirrel is around 5 to 10 years.

The hump of a camel is made of fat, not water.

The hissing sound of a snake comes from the air being pushed out through its mouth.

The average lifespan of a dragonfly is only about 24 hours.

A snail can sleep for up to three years.

Animals

The stripes on a zebra are as unique as human fingerprints.

The ears of a cricket are located on its front legs.

The eyes of an ostrich are bigger than its brain.

Dolphins use a special form of communication called echolocation to navigate and find food.

Wolves have a strong sense of smell and can detect scents up to 1.5 miles away.

The world's most popular animal in Australia is the kangaroo, which is a marsupial that is native to Australia.

Animals

Elephants are the largest land animals on Earth and can weigh as much as five cars.

A praying mantis can rotate its head almost 180 degrees.

The Glaucus Atlanticus, or the blue dragon, is a small sea slug that floats on the ocean's surface and feeds on venomous jellyfish.

The kakapo, a flightless parrot, is the heaviest parrot species in the world.

The mantis shrimp has incredibly powerful claws that can strike with the speed of a bullet, capable of breaking glass aquarium walls.

The mara, a rodent native to South America, resembles a cross between a rabbit and a deer.

Animals

The chameleon can change its color to match its surroundings.

Dolphins are known to be one of the smartest animals in the ocean and they communicate using a series of clicks and whistles.

The world's most popular animal in Africa is the lion, which is the king of the jungle.

Penguins are birds that cannot fly but are excellent swimmers, using their wings as flippers.

Platypuses are unique mammals that lay eggs and have bills similar to ducks.

Squirrels plant thousands of trees each year by forgetting where they buried their acorns.

Animals

Hyenas have a strong bite force and can even crack bones with their powerful jaws.

The honey badger is known for its fearless nature and ability to withstand venomous snake bites.

Flamingos are born with gray feathers and gradually turn pink due to the food they eat, which contains pigments called carotenoids.

Honeybees communicate with each other by dancing.

The toucan's beak is both lightweight and strong, allowing it to reach fruit on thin branches.

The anglerfish uses a glowing lure on top of its head to attract prey.

SPORTS

Sports

The sport of kabaddi originated in ancient India and is played without any equipment or gear.

Sepak takraw is a sport popular in Southeast Asia that combines elements of soccer and volleyball, and players use their feet to kick a rattan ball over a net.

Chess boxing is a unique sport that combines chess and boxing, where competitors alternate between rounds of chess and rounds of boxing.

In Bossaball, players combine elements of soccer, volleyball, and gymnastics while playing on an inflatable court with trampolines.

Jai alai is a sport originally from Spain that involves players using a curved basket called a cesta to sling a ball against a wall at high speeds.

Competitive cup stacking, also known as sport stacking, involves stacking plastic cups in specific sequences as quickly as possible.

Sports

Ultimate frisbee is a non-contact team sport where players pass a disc down the field in an effort to score points by catching it in the opposing team's end zone.

Tejo, a traditional Colombian sport, involves throwing metal discs at gunpowder-filled paper triangles to create explosions upon impact.

Equestrian vaulting is a discipline that combines gymnastics and dance performed on horseback.

Roller derby is a contact sport played on roller skates, with teams racing around an oval track and trying to score points by passing opponents.

Artistic cycling is a sport where athletes perform acrobatic tricks and balances on a fixed-gear bicycle.

The world's most popular sport is football, which is played by over 250 million people worldwide.

Sports

The world's most expensive sport is yacht racing, which can cost millions of dollars to participate in.

Calcio Storico is an ancient form of football played in Florence, Italy, where anything goes, including punching and wrestling.

Elephant polo is a variation of traditional polo played while riding elephants instead of horses.

Synchronized swimming combines elements of dance, gymnastics, and swimming to create a graceful and synchronized performance in water.

Blind soccer, also known as goalball, is played by visually impaired athletes using a ball with bells inside.

Ice yachting is a sport where participants sail across frozen lakes or rivers in boats fitted with ice skates.

Sports

The first basketball game was played in the United States in 1891.

The first golf game was played in Scotland in 1457.

In cricket, the longest match ever played lasted for 12 days.

Olympic gold medals are mostly made of silver, with only a thin layer of gold coating.

The world's oldest football club, Sheffield FC, was founded in England in 1857.

The first modern Olympic Games were held in Athens, Greece, in 1896.

Sports

The sport of surfing originated in ancient Polynesia.

Gymnastics was practiced in ancient Greece as a form of exercise and entertainment.

Taekwondo is a Korean martial art that emphasizes high, fast kicks.

In synchronized swimming, athletes must hold their breath for extended periods of time.

Pole vaulting is an athletic event that involves using a flexible pole to clear a high bar.

Karate is a martial art that originated in Okinawa, Japan.

Sports

Judo is a Japanese martial art that focuses on throws and grappling techniques.

Hurling, an Irish sport, is one of the oldest field games and is played with a wooden stick called a hurley.

Parkour is a discipline where athletes navigate urban environments by running, jumping, and climbing over obstacles.

Capoeira is a Brazilian martial art that combines elements of dance, acrobatics, and music.

Table tennis, also known as ping pong, became an Olympic sport in 1988.

Rodeo is a popular Western sport involving various events such as bull riding, barrel racing, and roping.

Sports

Dragon boat racing is a water sport originating from China, where teams paddle in long, narrow boats to the beat of a drum.

Yukigassen is a snowball fighting competition that originated in Japan, with teams battling to capture the opponent's flag.

Powerlifting is a strength sport where participants compete to lift the heaviest weight possible in three different lifts.

Calva is a traditional Mexican game similar to horseshoes, where players throw large metal rings at a target to score points.

The javelin used in track and field events is made from lightweight materials like carbon fiber.

Street luge is an extreme sport where participants lie down on a small sled and race downhill at high speeds.

Sports

Sepak bola api, also known as fireball soccer, is played with a flaming coconut instead of a regular ball.

Sumo wrestling is a Japanese sport where two wrestlers try to force each other out of a circular ring using their size and strength.

Tug of war is a team sport where two teams pull on opposite ends of a rope, trying to bring the center marker past a designated point to win.

The first Muay Thai match was held in Thailand in the 18th century.

Cricket is a popular sport in countries like England, India, and Australia.

Fencing is a combat sport that involves two competitors trying to touch each other with a sword.

Sports

The Olympic Games are held every four years and bring athletes from around the world together to compete.

Archery is one of the oldest sports in the world, dating back to ancient times.

Dodgeball is a game where you try to hit opponents with balls while avoiding being hit yourself.

Netball is a popular sport, especially among girls, which resembles basketball but has different rules.

Hapkido is a Korean martial art that focuses on self-defense techniques and joint locks.

The first hockey game was played in Montreal, Canada, in 1875.

FRUITS & VEGETABLES

Fruits & Vegetables

Apples come in many different colors, such as red, green, and yellow.

Did you know that strawberries are not really berries? They are actually considered a fruit.

Cucumbers are made up of about 95% water, so they can help keep you hydrated.

Watermelons are the perfect summer snack because they are juicy and refreshing.

Carrots are excellent for your eyesight because they contain a lot of vitamin A.

Oranges are an excellent source of vitamin C, which helps keep your immune system strong.

Fruits & Vegetables

The pineapple is a tropical fruit that grows on a plant and is known for its sweet and tangy taste.

Grapes come in different colors, such as green, red, and purple, and can be eaten fresh or turned into raisins.

Broccoli is a vegetable that looks like a small tree and is packed with vitamins and minerals.

Bananas are one of the most popular fruits in the world and are a great source of potassium.

Blueberries are tiny fruits that are rich in antioxidants, which can help protect your body from damage.

Pineapples contain an enzyme called bromelain, which can help with digestion.

Fruits & Vegetables

Spinach is a leafy green vegetable that is full of iron, which helps make your muscles strong.

Strawberries have tiny seeds on the outside, and each one is called an achene.

Cauliflower can be white, purple, or green and is a great source of vitamins and fiber.

Kiwis are small fruits with fuzzy brown skin and bright green flesh full of vitamin C.

Did you know that peppers belong to the same family as tomatoes, potatoes, and eggplants?

Limes are citrus fruits that are often used to add a tangy flavor to drinks and recipes.

Fruits & Vegetables

 Raspberries are delicate fruits that are known for their sweet and slightly tart taste.

 Celery is a crunchy vegetable that is low in calories and high in fiber.

 Mangoes are tropical fruits with a sweet and juicy flesh that is packed with vitamins and minerals.

 Asparagus is a long and slender vegetable that is often cooked and served as a side dish.

 Pineapples take about two years to grow before they are ready to be harvested.

 Did you know that olives are technically fruits? They are often used to make olive oil and are enjoyed in Mediterranean cuisine.

Fruits & Vegetables

Avocados are native to Mexico and Central America. They are a good source of healthy fats, fiber, and vitamins.

Celery is actually a stem vegetable. It is a good source of fiber and vitamin K.

Pomegranates can have more than 600 seeds inside them.

Watermelons are 92% water, making them a refreshing summer fruit.

Dragon fruit is native to Central and South America and belongs to the cactus family.

Artichokes are actually flower buds that haven't bloomed yet.

Fruits & Vegetables

The world's largest exporter of bananas is Ecuador.

Brazil is famous for producing a variety of delicious tropical fruits like mangoes and passion fruit.

Pineapples are commonly grown in tropical regions such as Hawaii, Thailand, and the Philippines.

Japan is known for cultivating small, sweet and seedless watermelons.

Oranges thrive in warm climates like those found in Florida and California.

Coconuts are abundant in countries with tropical coastlines, including Indonesia and the Philippines.

Fruits & Vegetables

India is a major producer of spices such as turmeric, ginger, and cinnamon.

Spain is known for its deliciously juicy and flavorful tomatoes.

Peru is famous for its unique purple corn, which is used to make a traditional drink called chicha morada.

Colombia is one of the largest exporters of coffee beans, known for its rich and aromatic flavor.

Egypt has a long history of cultivating dates, which have been grown along the Nile River for thousands of years.

The Netherlands is famous for its tulips, but it also exports large quantities of onions and potatoes.

Fruits & Vegetables

China is the largest producer of apples in the world, with numerous varieties grown across the country.

Greece is renowned for its flavorful olives and olive oil production.

The United States is a leading producer of corn, soybeans, and wheat.

Papayas are often referred to as "the fruit of the angels."

Potatoes are native to the Andes Mountains. They are a good source of carbohydrates, fiber, and vitamins.

The high altitudes of Ethiopia provide ideal conditions for growing flavorful coffee beans.

FLOWERS

Flowers

The world's smallest flower is called Wolffia and it's so tiny that it can fit on the head of a pin.

Orchids come in all shapes and sizes, including some that look like monkeys and dancing ladies.

Venus Flytraps are special plants that eat insects for their meals.

Violets are not only purple, but they can also be blue, yellow, or white.

Tulips were once more valuable than gold in the Netherlands.

The Lotus flower is sacred in many Asian cultures land represents purity and enlightenment.

Flowers

The Rafflesia flower is the largest in the world and can grow up to three feet in diameter!

Did you know that some flowers smell like chocolate? They're called Chocolate Cosmos.

Pitcher plants have leaves that form into pitcher-shaped traps to catch insects.

The Bluebell flower can only be found in certain parts of the world, like Europe and Asia.

Some types of lilies are toxic to cats, so be careful if you have a feline friend at home.

Carnations are not just pretty, they also have a spicy flavor that can be used in cooking.

Flowers

The Bleeding Heart flower has heart-shaped petals and looks like it's crying.

Did you know that the scent of lavender can help you relax and sleep better?

Hibiscus flowers are often used to make delicious teas and refreshing drinks.

Did you know that some species of roses can live for hundreds of years?

Daffodils are one of the first flowers to bloom in the spring, signaling the end of winter.

Lavender is not only fragrant but can also be used to make essential oils, soaps, and sachets.

Flowers

Water Lilies are aquatic plants that float on the surface of ponds and lakes, creating beautiful scenes.

The Morning Glory flower blooms early in the morning and closes by noon.

The Edelweiss flower is known for its woolly white petals and grows in the Alps.

The California Poppy is the official state flower of California and blooms in vibrant orange and yellow colors.

The Black Bat Flower gets its name from its dark, bat-shaped petals.

The world's most popular flower, the rose, is native to Europe and Asia. It is a symbol of love, beauty, and passion.

Flowers

Orchids are one of the oldest flower species on Earth and have been around for millions of years.

The Cherry Blossom Festival in Japan celebrates the arrival of spring and the beauty of cherry blossom trees.

The national flower of Mexico is the dahlia, which comes in vibrant colors like red, pink, and orange.

Violets can be used to make natural dyes for coloring fabrics and even food!

The flower of the hibiscus plant is the national flower of Malaysia and represents courage and power.

Did you know that some flowers, like the pansy, are edible and can be used in salads and desserts?

Flowers

Begonia flowers release water droplets from their leaves, causing them to shine like mirrors in the light.

Gazania flowers open under the sun and close towards the sky, resembling little suns in motion.

Dandelion flowers transform into fluffy seed heads known as "wishes" when they finish blooming, and blowing on them is said to make your wishes come true.

The world's most versatile flower, the tulip, is native to Central Asia. It can be used in gardens, bouquets, and as a food source.

The hollyhock flower can be made into dolls by attaching a flower for the body and a bud for the head.

Carnations are popular flowers for Mother's Day, symbolizing love and gratitude.

Flowers

Not all flowers are fragrant. Some flowers have no scent at all!

The color of a flower is determined by the pigments in its petals. Each pigment absorbs certain wavelengths of light, which determine the flower's color.

The flower of the cacao tree is only pollinated by tiny flies called midges.

The daisy is the most common flower in the world, with over 10,000 species.

The peony is a lush, fragrant flower that's often called the "queen of the garden."

White roses symbolize innocence and purity.

Flowers

There are over 32,000 types of flowers or flowering plants grown in North America.

Snowdrop flowers, peonies, and coneflowers grow best in some of the coldest places.

Peonies have been used as medicine for more than 2,000 years.

Chrysanthemums represent joy and happiness.

Hyacinths were named after a Greek mythological character.

Rosemary aids memory when the leaves are rubbed.

Flowers

Jasmine flowers need moonlight to release their scent.

Milkweed flowers contain a sticky juice that traps insects.

Malva flowers were used as food by the ancient Romans.

The colour blue in flowers attracts bees the most.

Bluebonnets grow only in central Texas and nearby areas.

Daffodils are planted on river banks to prevent soil erosion.

Flowers

Saffron crocus flowers are used to make the world's most expensive spice.

Water lilies close their petals at night to prevent animals from eating them.

Most flowers emit ethylene gas as they age which makes them wilt.

Morning glory vines will bend towards the sun as it rises.

Cosmos flowers represent peace and tranquility.

Wax plants were used as candle substitutes by early colonists.

Flowers

Star of Bethlehem flowers only appear every seven years.

Magnolia flowers only bloom for 10 days each year.

The daffodil is a sure sign of spring, and it's also the national flower of Wales.

The Bluebell flower is a symbol of humility in many cultures.

The Snapdragon flower resembles a dragon with its open mouth and often used in floral arrangements.

The African Daisy is a flower that closes at night and opens up in the morning, making it a great alarm clock for gardeners.

LANDMARKS

Landmarks

 The Leaning Tower of Pisa in Italy leans because of a soft foundation and was built over a period of almost 200 years.

 The Great Wall of China is actually a series of walls and fortifications built over hundreds of years to protect China from invaders.

 The Parthenon in Greece was built in honor of the goddess Athena and is one of the most famous examples of ancient Greek architecture.

 The Sphinx in Egypt has the body of a lion and the head of a human, and its purpose is still a mystery to archaeologists.

 The Moai statues on Easter Island are believed to have been created to honor ancestors and were carved by the Rapa Nui people between 1250 and 1500 CE.

 Stonehenge in England is a prehistoric monument believed to have been constructed between 3000 and 2000 BCE and is still a mystery to archaeologists.

Landmarks

The Colosseum in Rome was used for gladiatorial contests and other public spectacles and could hold up to 80,000 spectators.

The Eiffel Tower in Paris was originally built as a temporary exhibit for the 1889 World's Fair and was almost dismantled after the fair ended.

The Petra Treasury in Jordan is an ancient temple carved out of a sandstone cliff and is one of the most famous landmarks in the Middle East.

The Golden Gate Bridge in San Francisco is a suspension bridge that spans 1.7 miles (2.7 kilometers) and was completed in 1937.

The Tower Bridge in London is a bascule and suspension bridge that was completed in 1894 and is a symbol of the city.

The Machu Picchu in Peru is an ancient Incan citadel that was rediscovered in 1911 and is now a popular tourist destination.

Landmarks

The Chichen Itza in Mexico is an ancient Mayan city with impressive architectural features, including the famous El Castillo pyramid.

The Christ the Redeemer statue in Rio de Janeiro, Brazil is a 98-foot-tall statue of Jesus Christ that was completed in 1931.

The Alhambra in Spain is a palace and fortress complex that was built in the 13th century and is a UNESCO World Heritage Site.

The Sydney Opera House in Australia is a performing arts center with a distinctive design that resembles a series of sails.

The Palace of Versailles in France was the principal royal residence of France from 1682 until the French Revolution in 1789.

The Angkor Wat in Cambodia is a temple complex that was built in the 12th century and is the largest religious monument in the world.

Landmarks

The Tower of London in England has served as a royal palace, fortress, and prison over the centuries and is home to the Crown Jewels.

The Taj Mahal in India is a mausoleum built by Mughal Emperor Shah Jahan in memory of his wife Mumtaz Mahal.

The Palace of Westminster in London is home to the Houses of Parliament and is famous for its iconic clock tower, Big Ben.

The Acropolis in Athens, Greece is a UNESCO World Heritage Site and is home to several ancient ruins, including the Parthenon.

The Forbidden City in Beijing, China was the imperial palace of the Ming and Qing dynasties and is now a museum.

The Statue of Liberty in New York City was a gift from France to the United States and is a symbol of freedom and democracy.

Landmarks

The Tower of Hercules in Spain is an ancient lighthouse that has been in continuous use since the 2nd century AD.

The Palace of Mysore in India is a grand palace that was the residence of the Wodeyar dynasty and is now a museum.

The Mont Saint-Michel in France is a medieval abbey built on an island that is only accessible during low tide.

The Pantheon in Rome was originally built as a temple to all the gods and is known for its massive dome and impressive engineering.

The Golden Pavilion in Kyoto, Japan is a Buddhist temple covered in gold leaf and is known for its stunning reflection in the surrounding pond.

The Sistine Chapel in Vatican City is famous for its ceiling painted by Michelangelo, which depicts scenes from the Bible.

Landmarks

The Grand Tetons in Wyoming are a mountain range that is part of the Rocky Mountains and is known for its stunning scenery and wildlife.

The Mona Lisa painting by Leonardo da Vinci is housed in the Louvre Museum in Paris, France and is one of the most famous paintings in the world.

The Colossus of Rhodes was a statue of the Greek god Helios and stood over 100 feet (30 meters) tall before it was destroyed by an earthquake in 226 BCE.

The Salar de Uyuni in Bolivia is the largest salt flat in the world and is known for its otherworldly landscape.

The Victoria Falls in Zambia and Zimbabwe is one of the largest waterfalls in the world, with a width of over a mile (1.7 kilometers).

The Potala Palace in Lhasa, Tibet is a massive palace complex that was the residence of the Dalai Lama until 1959.

Landmarks

The White House in Washington, D.C. is the official residence of the President of the United States and has been in use since 1800.

The Eiger in Switzerland is a famous mountain peak that is known for its challenging climbing routes.

The Cenotes in Mexico are natural swimming holes that were formed by the collapse of limestone bedrock, creating a unique and beautiful landscape.

The Fairy Chimneys in Turkey are towering rock formations that were formed by volcanic activity and erosion, creating a surreal and magical landscape.

The Salar de Atacama in Chile is one of the driest places on Earth and is home to stunning salt flats and colorful lagoons.

The Hill of Crosses in Lithuania is a hill covered in thousands of crosses, each representing a prayer or wish.

Landmarks

The Door County Sea Cave in Wisconsin, United States is a series of sea caves that are only accessible by water and contain stunning rock formations.

The Door of the Lions in Spain is a giant stone arch that was once the entrance to a medieval castle.

The Pink Lake in Western Australia gets its color from algae that produce a red pigment.

The Giant Buddha in Leshan, China is the largest statue of Buddha in the world, carved into a cliff face.

The Eye of the Sahara in Mauritania is a mysterious geological formation that looks like a giant bullseye from space.

The Red Beach in China is a beach covered in red seaweed that turns the entire beach red during the autumn months.

SCIENCE

Science

The human nose can detect over 1 trillion different scents!

The universe is still expanding, and the rate of this expansion is accelerating!

The largest planet in our solar system is Jupiter, which is more than 1,300 times the size of Earth.

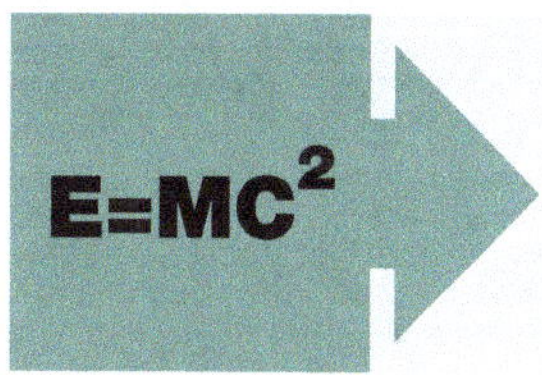

The highest mountain in our solar system is Olympus Mons on Mars, which is three times the height of Mount Everest.

The human eye can distinguish between over 10 million different colors!

The fastest-growing plant in the world is the bamboo, which can grow up to 1 meter in just 24 hours.

Science

The Earth's atmosphere is about 78% nitrogen, 21% oxygen, and 1% other gases.

The Earth's oceans contain about 97% of the planet's water.

Venus spins backwards compared to other planets in our solar system.

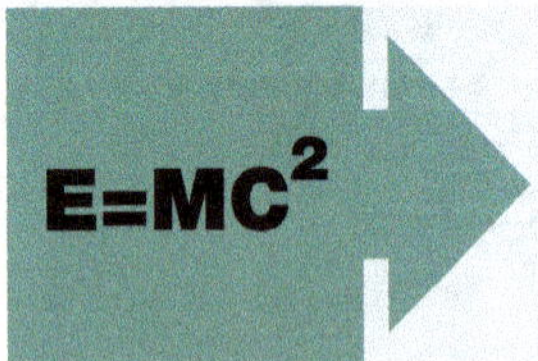

Some frogs can actually freeze solid in winter and then thaw out in spring, returning back to life.

Giraffes only sleep for about two hours a day.

Whales communicate at a lower frequency than humans can hear.

Science

Snails can sleep for up to 3 years without eating.

The smallest bone in the human body is located in your ear.

The sloth takes two weeks to digest their food.

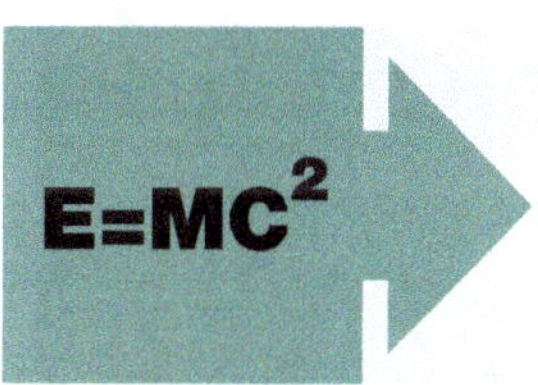

Koalas sleep for up to 22 hours a day. When they are awake they mostly just eat eucalyptus leaves.

Pigs can't look up into the sky. The shape of their eye sockets prevent them from doing so.

A goldfish has a memory span of only 3 seconds.

Science

Volcanoes can produce more than 500 kinds of gases, including water vapor, carbon dioxide, sulfur dioxide and hydrogen chloride.

Astronauts in space grow taller for a while due to the absence of gravity pulling them down.

Coffee wakes you up because caffeine blocks a certain chemical that makes you sleepy.

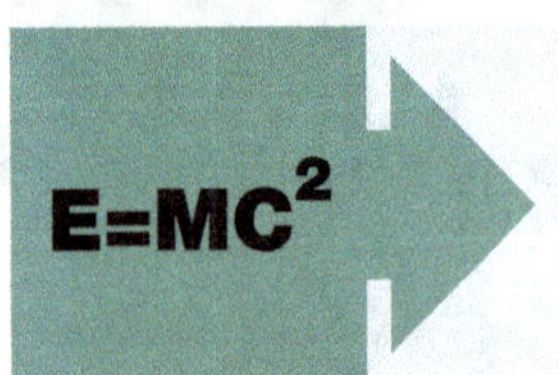

Raindrops evaporate before they reach the ground in hot deserts.

Silver has the highest electrical and thermal conductivity of all metals.

A rabbit's front teeth never stop growing. They keep wearing down as the rabbit chews to keep them at a usable length.

Science

The ozone layer in our atmosphere helps protect the surface of Earth from harmful ultraviolet radiation emitted by the Sun.

Dolphins sleep with one eye open! They only sleep with half of their brain at a time so they can still surface to breathe.

Bacteria can double their numbers every 20 minutes under ideal conditions. This is why bacterial infections can spread rapidly inside the body.

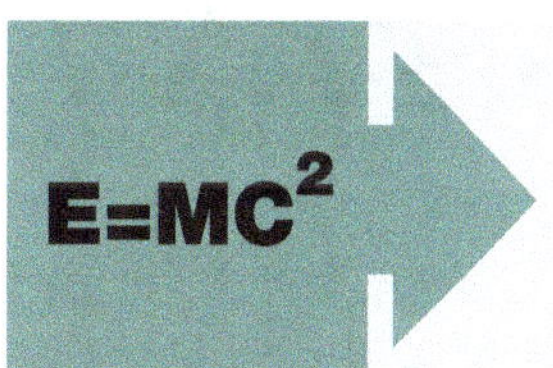

Coffee beans are actually seeds, so when these "beans" are roasted and ground, the result is ground seed tissue that we infuse with hot water to make coffee.

An octopus has three hearts! Two pump blood through its gills while the third sends blood to the rest of its body.

Trees give off water through their leaves in a process called transpiration. They draw up water from their roots and release excess water as vapor.

Science

Baby teeth fall out to make room for permanent adult teeth. They also help children learn how to chew different types of food.

Hot air balloons rise because hot air is less dense than cold air, so it is pushed up by the denser cold air below it.

Helium is the only element that cannot be made to freeze at room temperature, no matter how cold you make it. It remains a gas.

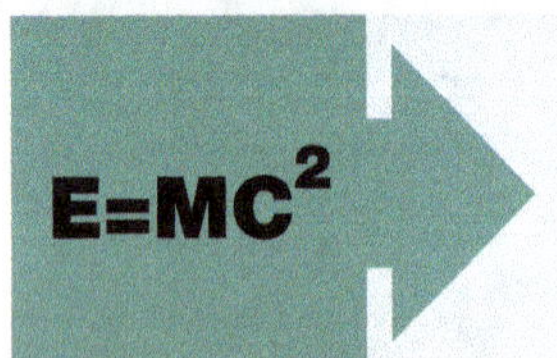

The human eye can process 36,000 bits of information every hour.

The human brain uses over 20% of the body's energy, even though it only makes up about 2% of the body's weight.

The human body contains enough iron to make a small nail.

Science

The first recorded use of the word "science" was in 1834.

The first dinosaur fossil was discovered in 1824 in England.

The first successful organ transplant was a kidney in 1954.

A group of spiders can spin silk that is stronger than steel, relative to its weight.

A fossil is the hardened remains of an animal or plant from long ago trapped in rock.

The first electric car was built in 1832 by Robert Anderson.

JOBS

Jobs

There's a job called "snake milker" where you have to extract venom from snakes to make medicine.

A "Fruit Taster" gets to taste test fruits to determine their quality and ripeness.

Wildlife photographers wait patiently for weeks to get the perfect shot of an animal.

Window cleaners climb up to 1,500 feet to clean the windows of skyscrapers.

Airline pilots can fly up to 15 hours straight during long-haul flights.

Lifeguards train for months to perfect their rescue techniques.

Jobs

Dentists sterilize their tools after treating each patient.

Cartoonists can draw over 500 drawings in a single work day.

Barbers cut over 20 heads of hair per workday.

Teachers grade over 100 assignments every workweek.

Gardeners prune over 100 plants in a single day of work.

Cashiers handle over 500 banknotes as part of their daily work.

Jobs

Translators translate over 100,000 words annually.

Waiters carry over 100 kilograms of food trays in a single work shift.

The average person changes jobs 12 times in their lifetime.

Glaziers design and cut glass to reflect certain wavelengths of light.

Foresters identify over 500 species of trees through sight and smell.

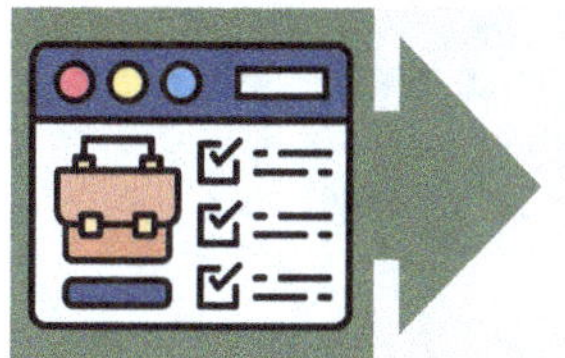

Pilots speak over 10 codes and phrases to air traffic control that outsiders don't understand.

Jobs

Lego brick artists can create anything from small sculptures to life-size replicas of famous landmarks using thousands of Lego bricks.

Mushroom pickers must have extensive knowledge of different types of mushrooms and be able to distinguish between edible and poisonous varieties.

Farmers learn the growth habits and weaknesses of over 50 types of crops.

Musicians play extremely quietly to detect weaknesses or out of tune notes.

Lego brick artists may also create commissioned pieces for businesses or private collectors.

A "Snowmaker" creates artificial snow for ski resorts and winter sports.

MUSIC
MUSICAL INSTRUMENTS

Musical Instruments

The oboe was once used to imitate the sound of crying doves in performances.

The harp strings are plucked instead of bowed, producing a melodious sound.

The pan flute can produce more than one note at a time due to its multiple joined pipes.

The electric guitar amplifies strings vibrations using an electromagnetic pickup system.

The ukulele is derived from the Portuguese instrument of the same name brought to Hawaii in 1879.

The clarinet has a single reed that vibrates when air is blown through a hollow wooden tube.

Musical Instruments

The glass harmonica is made up of spinning glass bowls that create a hauntingly beautiful sound.

The mandolin is a small, stringed instrument that is commonly used in folk music.

The nyckelharpa is a Swedish stringed instrument with 16 strings that are played with a bow.

The koto is a Japanese stringed instrument that is played with finger picks and produces a delicate, melodic sound.

The piano is one of the most popular musical instruments in the world, with over 10 million pianos sold each year.

The saxophone was invented by a man named Adolphe Sax in the 1840s. He wanted to create an instrument that would be a hybrid of the clarinet and the brass horn.

Musical Instruments

The French horn is a brass instrument that is played by blowing air through a mouthpiece, producing a mellow and rich sound.

The oboe is a woodwind instrument that is played by blowing air through a reed, producing a sharp and clear sound.

The sitar is a stringed instrument from India that is played by plucking the strings with a plectrum, producing a unique and complex sound.

The rainstick is a percussion instrument that produces a sound similar to rainfall and is made from a hollowed-out cactus stem filled with pebbles or beans.

The guiro is a Latin American instrument made from a hollowed-out gourd.

The tuba is a brass instrument that produces deep and low sounds.

Musical Instruments

The harp is considered to be the oldest string instrument, dating back to at least 3000 B.C.

The word "organ" comes from the Greek word "organon," meaning "instrument."

The electric guitar was invented in 1931 by George Beauchamp and Adolph Rickenbacker.

The harmonica is held horizontally in the left hand while the right hand operates the bellows and covers holes.

The word "jazz" originally referred to improvised music and the instruments associated with it.

Piano strings are made of either plain or phosphor bronze wire or high tensile steel wire.

Musical Instruments

The violin family consists of the violin, viola, cello and double bass.

Instruments like the violin, cello, guitar and piano became extremely popular in Europe during the 19th century.

Studies show playing an instrument can reduce stress, improve sleep and boost self-confidence in children.

The accordion is a keyboard instrument that is played by pressing buttons or keys, which makes a sound.

The xylophone is a percussion instrument that is played by hitting metal bars with a mallet, which produces a sound.

The bagpipes are a wind instrument that is played by blowing air into a bag, which produces a distinctive sound.

Musical Instruments

The marimba is a percussion instrument that is played by striking wooden bars with a mallet, which produces a bright sound.

The piano is a versatile instrument that can be used to play many different styles of music, from classical to jazz to pop.

The guitar was originally made with 4 strings but was expanded to 6 strings during the Renaissance.

Ancient trumpets were traditionally made of animal horns or seashells.

A violin bow uses between 50–100 horse hairs to produce sound.

A ukulele is a version of a small guitar that originated in Portugal.

Musical Instruments

The oldest saxophone was made in 1846.

Bells produce sound due to metal vibrations rather than strings or air.

The word "guitar" originated from the Arabic word "qitara."

Marimbas originated in Africa and spread to Latin America.

Different sizes of harps produce different ranges of notes.

The sound hole on a guitar helps transmit string vibrations to the air.

Musical Instruments

Playing the trumpet requires using the lips, teeth and tongue to produce different notes.

Violins in their modern form became popular in the 17th and 18th centuries in Italy.

Humans have played sitars for at least 1,500 years originating in ancient India.

Europeans started playing lutes at least 1,200 years ago during the Middle Ages.

Egyptians played harps at least 3,500 years ago during the Old Kingdom era.

The classical guitar was developed in Spain in the early 19th century.

Musical Instruments

Violins have an average of 250 separate parts in their construction.

Saxophones often go out of tune after just 15 minutes of playing.

Trumpets look like they would be easy to play but require extreme lip control and endurance.

The first violin was invented by accident when a fiddler dropped his instrument into a pot of glue.

Saxophones were originally marketed as health products for curing bronchitis and asthma.

Trumpets were originally used to give commands on the battlefield rather than play melodies.

Musical Instruments

Guitars were first developed from old fishing nets that fishermen strummed while at sea.

Flutes were first used to imitate animal and bird calls before being used to play melodies.

Wind instruments were dismissed as rude and unable to play with subtlety through antiquity.

Ukuleles were mocked as toy guitars incapable of serious musical expression until recently.

Playing the violin can trigger the same area of the brain responsible for speech production.

Guitar players often develop hardened, thickened skin on the tip of their left hand's index finger.

Musical Instruments

The piano was developed in Italy during the Renaissance period.

Playing music can lower your stress hormone levels by up to 30%.

Learning an instrument can boost creative thinking skills in children.